It changed my life...

It's like nothing I've tried before...   Sara Alshareef

Inspiring & motivating...   Genna Louise-Ingold

I don't understand how she does it. Amazing...   Yulya Tretyakova

She went straight to the root of the problem   Alja Belova

Credible & engaging...   Sharon Loeschen

She works on so many different levels...   Melanie Watters

Inspiring...   Marianne Craig

ENRICH

Your Relationships:

10 SECRETS TO REKINDLE YOUR

INTIMATE LIFE

by Darya Haitoglou

This book is intended as an informational guide. The remedies, approaches, and techniques described herein are meant to supplement, and not to be a substitute for, professional medical care or treatment. They should not be used for a serious ailment without prior consultation with a qualified healthcare professional.

Printed in the United Kingdom

10 9 8 7 6 5 4 3 2 1

Library of Congress Cataloging-in-Publication Data

Haitoglou, Darya; Enrich Your Relationships: 10 Secrets To Rekindle Your Intimate Life, ISBN-13: 978-1515095347, ISBN-10: 1515095347

Summary: This practical book is for anyone looking to re-evaluate their communication style and take their relationship to a deeper, more intimate level. Full of advice, research and case-studies, the book also contains a selection of life-changing exercises that can be undertaken in a matter of minutes. This guide is highly recommended for couples who struggle to balance their work, life and relationship cycles, new parents, those in long-term partnerships and individuals or couples with intimacy issues. It will also benefit anyone searching for their soulmate or those that simply strive to create happy relationships from the start and transform their intimacy into a positive and fruitful experience.

www.enrichyourrelationships.com

Dedicated to my soulmate and partner Alexander and our children Dimitri and Nikolai.

May you live your lives to the fullest and feel enriched and blessed in many ways.

PREFACE

Your Inner Diamond

When I was 14 years old, I saw a poster in my home city that was for a workshop called 'Increase Your Confidence', and like most of teens, I was interested in doing so. Before that event, I had very low self-esteem. I had very few real friends. I was bullied at school, and I had a skin condition that was so visible that I was ashamed of my body. I was shy about embarking on any meaningful relationships and focused mainly on myself. After undertaking the training, I immediately felt a sense of freedom and gratitude as the words and techniques I had witnessed not only impacted me on that day but genuinely for the rest of my life. I would dearly love to see every school offering their students this type of workshop since we now live in a world of virtual reality, fake identities, celebrity culture and superficial communication. Being the *true You* is vital. It is essential to feel good about yourself and young adults are the ones who, I believe, suffer the most. At the core is how to stay feeling beautiful, lovable, worthy, able, and capable of whatever we want to do. Ultimately, be true to ourselves and decide what you want. To start this journey, we all need to see our own and each other's inner worth. This will help enrich relationships and create more congruent families who are happy, love-rich, and blame-free.

With love & gratitude,

Darya

Contents

INTRODUCTION

"The easiest kind of relationship is with ten thousand people, the hardest is with one." - Joan Baez

According to many psychologists, the average lifespan of the 'falling in love' stage is about two years. Once this time has passed, often the magic wears off and people are left disappointed. They may even start looking for new bonds as they question the very essence of love. But what is 'love'?

Some people say that love is something ephemeral, unpredictable, and unexplainable. Hard to get and hard to keep. They say it is like a 'fairy mist' that casts the spell on one another.

Some believe that it comes from God and that prayer makes it perfect. Some believe that love is the essence of life and its spiritual purpose.

Some believe that love is when you find the perfect match and then jump from partner to partner searching for 'true' love. In this case, what mostly happens is that they find themselves 'falling in love' again and again.

The truth is, when we understand that our emotions have a biological, hormonal explanation including 'falling in love' and 'being in love', it suddenly makes more sense. Science has already answered questions on who our ideal partner could be and how to find a soulmate based on our hormonal cocktail. Take, for example, the research by Dr Helen Fisher on four types of hormonal circuits that are evolutionary wired within us: dopamine, serotonin, testosterone, and oestrogen. According to her anthropological case studies of long-term relationships, people with a leading dopamine circuit are called EXPLORERS. They are risk-takers, adventurous, spontaneous, can easily go into extremes of happiness and despair, lovers of change, travel, and life in general. These EXPLORERS find their ideal partner from their own group.

The opposite of EXPLORERS are BUILDERS. They are loyal, reliable, pragmatic, traditional, conservative, stable and predictable. BUILDERS are led by a serotonin circuit. They find their ideal partner from their own group too.

DIRECTORS have a leading testosterone circuit. They are dominating, decision-makers, leaders and managers of others and are strong-willed. Their ideal match is not from their own group but from the last set known as NEGOTIATORS.

NEGOTIATORS, oestrogen-led circuit people, who are empathetic, social, friendly, amiable, and emotionally in-touch. They are mostly attracted by and to DIRECTORS. For more details, watch Helen's TED talk.

Her simple explanation is that if we knew what type of person was our 'ideal partner' we would not make as many bad relationship choices. In other words, there would be less family break-ups and more healthy and fruitful long-term partnerships.

My limited experience extends to two marriages, but I can support this research with practice. According to Fisher's research I am an EXPLORER and NEGOTIATOR, and my first husband was a BUILDER and a little bit of an EXPLORER. So it was a mismatch. When we first met, I thought that we were similar (EXPLORER talking) but when we started living together, I realised he was very traditional, loyal, and practical (BUILDER). Our marriage didn't work out. Guess what, eventually I found my ideal partner, an EXPLORER-DIRECTOR who is perfect for my EXPLORER-NEGOTIATOR personality. We have been living happily ever after.

So, the first point is that you need to set up a good foundation and have a partnership that is hormonally & values-matching, otherwise you must work harder on making your relationship work!

Also, there are times when there are high stress levels (e.g., a difficult event in life), when we need to get into balance. We need some tools to help us get into shape emotionally, mentally, and spiritually. Those who have lived in marriages for a long time, even with 'ideal partners,' know that at times help is needed and help is needed fast. Often, we are subconsciously looking for someone to learn secrets from about how to enrich relationships so we can take those gems and apply them to our life. At times, I wished that I had a compilation of some helpful strategies when I needed them to go through tough bits of my life. With this in mind, I have written this book.

So, to make it easier for you, the reader, secrets are in fact exercises and they are split into six chapters. I have included one or two in each chapter for the beginner's level. They are simple to do, and you can apply them in your everyday life. For those who are ready for more, there is an advanced guide with 50 more exercises.

To make it even simpler and to help you get started, you can begin with a questionnaire to help clarify which chapter you should start with. You can find the ENRICH questionnaire at the back of the book.

Why this book

I believe every person has a diamond inside them which is covered in dirt. This is like any diamond that is underneath the ground hiding amongst other rocks. Generally, people don't like to show the dirt that surrounds their diamond, so they create a sugary coating to sustain and hide all that is inside it. The cover that they like to show to the world is not really them. It's their mask that they have learnt to put on in order not to feel hurt. Because sometime in the past someone told them they were not good enough, or they were not worthy enough to be who they are, and they needed to become someone else. Someone better. Probably these beliefs were made with the best intention to protect that diamond but became no longer useful for a person in their adulthood. To feel free and for the soul to grow, we need to clean that diamond from the dirt around it. Quite simply, one needs to crack through the sugary crust. It is not comfortable, and it is not beautiful to allow dark, private stuff to slip out of a good-looking sugary crust, but it is paramount in order to **allow the diamond to be clean, so it radiates and shines**! This is the art of life and the most important thing I believe we live for. To be honest I love helping to crack that crust and have people polish that diamond and feel their diamond's worth. I always intend to raise their worth and with that, their self-esteem.

What I regularly see in my coaching and training practice is that 9 out of 10 people undervalue themselves. My bet is that you also undervalue your diamond. And what we want to do here, while you are reading this book, is to help you raise your self-esteem and see, clean, and polish your inner diamond.

Structure of this book

In my life so far, I have had the privilege of working with many experts in the field of psychology, family and couple therapy, neuro-linguistics and coaching, neuro-science, quantum-physics and much more. Throughout my quest to raise my own self-esteem, accept my identity and find my destiny, I have travelled the world and participated in coaching and training programmes for myself in order to learn from the best in the field. From this, I have practiced and condensed the many strategies that I have learnt over the course of my life into a simple structure to help people raise their self-esteem and achieve the relationships they've always wanted. What came out of this collection was an experiential workshop and then an ENRICHing programme that consisted of workshops, coaching and retreats. Working with families and couples and analysing what makes them happy and love-rich, I noticed that some strategies and exercises were helping better than others. The items that helped the most were learning to love yourself, stopping the blaming of others and communicating in a different way to live a happier life. As I was putting the structure of big topics into relationship bands, such as; Explore vs. routine, Nourish vs. deplete, Respond vs. react, Imagine vs. willpower, Communicate vs. assume, Hug & Humour vs. withdraw, I realised that they all fitted in the word ENRICH. So I kept them and now run workshops based on this structure. They have also become the titles of the six chapters in this book.

Chapter 1. Explore vs. routine

Chapter 2. Nourish vs. deplete

Chapter 3. Respond vs. react

Chapter 4. Imagine vs. willpower

Chapter 5. Communicate vs. assume

Chapter 6. Hug & humour vs. withdraw

In this book you will find transcribed interviews and stories of clients. Names have been changed, but the stories are real. I hope these practical examples help you to see your relationships from a different angle and learn what you need to do to allow your diamond to shine brighter.

You can start at any exercise in this book. Give yourself a chance to be surprised. Then you can decide which tools are best for you. Even if you only regularly apply one of these tools in your life, you will experience amazing shifts.

Why intimate relationships?

Statistics are quite alarming on intimate relationships. In many Western countries the divorce rate already sits at above 50%, like the USA (53%), France (55%), Spain (61%) whilst divorce in Belgium is now at a staggering 70%! [i]

And I can understand why. Generally, we are not taught at school nor at university on how to make a marriage work. The model shown by our parents is no longer valid in current times. Many of our families are dysfunctional and we sometimes don't have role models if our parents are divorced or have been abusive. So it is hard. I wish I had known some basic facts about relationships and how to enrich them when I was choosing my partners. I learnt by trial and error, but it doesn't mean everyone needs to! I wish I could read *Anatomy of Love* by Helen Fischer or visit Esther Perel's office for a session. I thought I was able to do it all myself, but the reality is that we cannot change a system from within. We need to reach out for help to gather some outside perspective.

Thanks...

If you're gonna tell your life story, you gotta be honest, or don't do it.

— R. Kelly

It feels strange that I'm writing this book. I had always thought I was better at mathematics than with words, and I studied economics because I thought the written language was too difficult for me. Obviously, that belief is no longer in my head.

This book is largely about the beliefs we have about ourselves and what relationships we are having, want to have or 'should' be having. I put 'should' in brackets as it is probably something we have learnt as a model from the culture and environment we grew up in, and most probably from our parents. I believe in saying 'thank you' to our parents and saying (even without saying to them) 'I have grown up now and can make my own decisions and I make choices that I believe are good for me. I've learnt a lot from the two of you and it is time for me to build the relationships I believe I want to have in my life the way I feel are right for me'. It took me some time to say that and life has simply catered for the rest.

Meanwhile, I would like to thank the many people who are in my life, and by just being there. They have contributed to this book.

Firstly, my parents, Olga and Yury. I love them dearly and I know they have been the best parents for me.

I also thank my sister Polina who I cherish. I think she is an amazing human being. She has inspired me in so many ways.

I thank from the bottom of my heart my husband, partner and soulmate, Alexander. I feel so proud we are together and for what he achieves in his life.

I would also like to thank my teachers and my friends who provide daily inspiration. Sharon Loeschen & Marianne Craig for continuous mentorship support and invaluable feedback. Victoria Stanford, Tracey Tannenbaum and the LitCrit Team for the editing of the book. Julia Seyatelevaya & Melanie Watters for giving precious feedback. Natalya Kharitonova for illustrations. Katerina Mavroedi for the design of the book cover. And every person who I have worked with and who has crossed my path.

Last, but not the least, I thank the participants of my workshops, my clients and you, the reader of this book. I wish for the best things to happen in your life and by being the best version of yourself, you can make your relationships and this world a better place.

Now, let's board the train for our journey into enriching relationships and start releasing those blocks and fears.

Go gather those new tools and strategies to enjoy the life and relationships you have been longing for.

CHAPTER ONE

Explore vs. routine

"Time to open up a new chapter in life, and to explore a larger centre." - Lillian Russell

OK, YOU MAY THINK, EXPLORE WHAT? I know this person inside-out and I can't seem to see any possibilities for improvement. You may be right, but the odds are that most probably you know your partner very little and even less than you think you do.

Let's have a look at this story.

Lucy and Mark are having a joint session and I ask each of them how well they think they know each other. On a scale of 0 to 10, Mark thinks he knows Lucy 6 out of 10. Lucy, on the other hand, says Mark knows her only 2 out of 10. They are both surprised with the outcome and curious to find out why.

The best thing is to ask yourself now, on a scale of 0 to 10, how well do you think you know your partner? And then, ask your partner what they think, and how much they think you know them on a scale of 0 to 10. Be ready to hear what they will say.

The feeling of 'I know him/her inside-out' comes generally from the feelings of routine in relationships. If this happens, she/he will do that, say this and it's probably going to be like that. You can trace this back to the evolution of your intimate life. It was initially exciting, but after a while, weeks, months, or years (this depends on different people) you may have grown to expect and settle for a more established routine. Then my question to you is: 'How much do you explore in intimacy?'

Most of the families, especially when they have children, find that routines help them organise their life and stay sane with demanding priorities of the family members. Routines bring sanity to the relationships, but routines can also bring boredom.

People can start feeling stale in their relationships because of these well-travelled routines.

Exploration, according to many relationship therapists, is a key to a happy relationship. If you are in a relationship that you want to transform or improve, you need to find new ways of dealing with issues that you have. Otherwise, following the same 'routine' or behavioural patterns will produce the same results you've been having. Even Albert Einstein once said, "It is insane to keep doing the same thing over and over again and expect different results." If you keep doing what you have been doing in an unhappy relationship, you will keep getting what you have been getting.

The questions are how to change the negative pattern of routine, mundane relationships and how to start exploring new avenues? There are multiple ways to start exploration in relationships. Below is one of the options.

I encourage you to do it at least once and make a little note (ideally on something like a Post-it note) what the outcome was. Place this note somewhere visible and leave it up for a week. There is enough evidence to suggest that when you write things down you subliminally store and retain the information for longer, which in turn allows you stick to something for an extended period of time.

Exercise 1. The first exercise for couples comes from Milton Erickson, a master who connects with people on a deeper level. Milton had polio and spent most of his time in a wheelchair observing people and their styles of behaviour. He also noticed that if he started breathing the same way as his patient, he established a quicker and more meaningful rapport, so he used this technique automatically in his psychotherapeutic practice. This comes as no surprise to many people who use this technique. It works because it is part of our human nature. We all have *mirror-neurons* and use them to tune in to understand the other person,

empathise with them and build enriching relationships.

Story:

Here is one of the examples of how it worked for Jenny in relation to her partner Tom:

Jenny: *"I wanted to tell you how much easier it was for me to talk to Tom when I tuned into his breathing. It was like being a different me! I don't think he noticed at the beginning, but when he arrived home, I was all stressed as I was expecting a rough discussion about his upcoming long-term trip abroad. I was nervous about how I would react to him telling me this as we haven't had time together for ages. I felt it would make it worse for us and was anxious that eventually it might result in a separation. I had lots of different fears as I was desperate to feel better.*

I started breathing like he did and just listened to what he was saying. I didn't go into my head interpreting and thinking of potential consequences, but instead just stayed there breathing with him. It took me a few moments and it worked! He was surprised and said that he was not expecting that type of discussion. I was calm. I was supportive of his trip. I nodded to him when he was talking, and I didn't feel angry or sad, which I normally feel when we talk. I think I have changed my own attitude to the whole thing.

I will keep doing this breath-tuning for all my big discussions with him from now on!"

The next time you see your partner, explore your breathing. Breathe with the same rhythm, speed and sound as your partner and see what happens. You will start tuning into each other and understanding each other better. Also, start mirroring your partner in gestures, posture and facial expressions. Ok, don't do it too obviously, but in a subtle way and the results will bring you a beautiful deep connection. Notice how they speak and adjust your speech accordingly. If they are using a high pitch voice, notice that and adjust yours to sound organically like theirs. If their speed is faster or slower, adjust yours. If their tone is louder or softer, change your tone to match theirs. I look forward to hearing how it worked for you and what changes it brought to your relationships.

Exercise 2. The second challenge focuses on you and your everyday life. When you wake up, start the day with a different routine. If you are used to something, change the sequence. For example, brush your teeth with the other hand or style your hair differently, put your watch on the other wrist or experiment with a new look using your existing clothes. It seems trivial but all the above can have a profound effect on your whole day and even the way you think! I challenge you to keep that change for at least three days. So if you change your watch to a different hand, keep it there for at least three days in order to have a sustainable effect on your brain.

Story:

Here is an example of what Margarita did.

Margarita: "I noticed that I started saying a phrase 'you know' too often with everyone I spoke to and it became kind of a parasite in my speech. So I decided to work on that by changing a routine. In the morning, I would normally put a band on my hair, but this time I put it on my wrist. Every time I noticed saying 'you know', I would pull the elastic band to remind myself of that bad habit. So it served both purposes for me, I changed my routine with the hair band and also helped myself to get rid of a bad habit.

TRY THIS:

Step 1. Choose what you want to change in your daily routine.

Step 2. Decide on an action reminder, i.e., when you wake up, put a note on an alarm as a reminder to complete the action.

Step 3. Stick to this new routine for at least three days to feel the difference. To be honest, you will probably still want to change it back (that's how strong an old habit pulls). For many people it takes 21+ days to change a habit, so if you want to really stick to it, do it for three weeks. This not only represents a good challenge for you but is a start to making a positive shift in your relationships, as your brain would have learnt a new pattern of exploring different things. This in turn will have a subtle and positive impact on other aspects of your life.

CHAPTER TWO

Nourish vs. deplete

"Criticism, like rain, should be gentle enough to nourish a man's growth without destroying his roots." - Frank A. Clark

"You cannot make a flower grow by jerking on it." - Virginia Satir.

TO NOURISH MEANS TO GIVE UNCONDITIONALLY. It's what Tom Rath and Donald Clifton wrote in *How Full is Your Bucket?* Based on the Gallup research, nourishment fills up an emotional bank account. People have emotional accounts with different emotional overdraft amounts depending on many factors such as their parents' model of behaviour, basic condition of their physical and emotional resilience levels, environment, beliefs, etc. (I won't go into details on these factors as it would take another book to write!). For some, it is very little before they start to feel depleted, for others, the overdraft is a bit larger. In relationships it's the same. There is a point where the water 'bucket' gets empty and if there is another thirsty person, no empathy is possible at that moment and a conflict for basic resources arises. So, how do we make sure we keep ourselves nourished instead of depleted?

It's important to understand the following. When going through a tough phase of your relationship, you first need to nourish yourself. If you are experiencing a rocky part of your life, it's like having a 'bucket' with a hole in it. First, you need to take time to mend it and then start filling it with water. Before an emotional storm, prepare and do your homework by nourishing yourself and your partner to make sure both of you have your full 'buckets'.

The best way to fill your 'bucket' is to raise your self-esteem. Now, this may sound difficult to do. We can have a full seminar on the topic alone, but I would like to give you one of effective exercises to start practicing.

Exercise 3. Nourish your body. Start your day early, earlier than normal by awaking and participating in some sort of physical activity, be it; yoga, stretching, pilates, jogging, dance, or anything that you enjoy that allows you to feel strong, relaxed and empowered. It's so important to give you, your body, and your mind a boost of energy first thing in the morning. Then, follow the activity with a contrast shower, warm and hot at the beginning and a blast of cold water at the end. Complete Exercise 3 with a self-massage to relax and rejuvenate.

Story:

Anna comes to the first session looking down, not smiling and her eyes look red.

Anna: I feel tired. I feel exhausted. I did all the checks with the doctor, and they are normal. I should be able to run my day fine, but I can't. I know I have a family and kids, but I just want to stay in bed all day long. I feel wiped out.

Me: What I hear is that you feel tired even before the day starts. And on a physical level your test results are fine. It is the feeling you have - you seem to want to stay in bed all day long because you feel tired.

Anna: Yes, and I wish I could just jump up and do all the things that I need to do to feel good about myself, about me being a mother, being a wife.

Me: Did you just say 'jump' up? By the way, what physical activity do you do in the morning? When was the last time you exercised?

Anna: A long time ago and I tried to go to the gym, but I hated it and it was far from home. I need to be close to my little kids.

Me: Yes, you want to be close to your kids and if you want to do exercises, where would that be ideally?

Anna: Ideally at home.

Me: Home. And what time of the day are you more likely to do the exercises?

Anna: Morning. Before the kids wake up. Once they are awake, I am running around like a headless chicken.

Me: In the morning, it looks like you are already running around the house, which sounds like some sort of physical activity.

Anna: Stretching would do me a lot of good as I have a sore back and shoulders. I could do it in the other room in the house. I could have a YouTube yoga video to exercise to and help me stay on track.

Two weeks later Anna is back to her normal energy level, and she even persuaded her partner to sign up to a gym. She also mentioned in the following session that this change of a routine on its own changed her relationship with her husband. They felt closer physically as they exercised together and supported each other mentally to keep themselves motivated.

One of the simplest ways to embark on a physical activity programme is to start small e.g., 10-20 minutes every day, to establish the habit. After a while, you will start to see and feel the amazing results and will automatically want to increase the time and length of your activity programme. Here is a great example – feel free to try. Search for '30 Day Yoga Challenge' with Erin Motz on Youtube. It is a free sequence of yoga videos for 30 days to stay fit. What a wonderful way to nourish yourself and to start a beautiful day every day!

Exercise 4. The next exercise is called '*5 Love languages*' and it comes from Gary Chapman. Basically, to nourish your relationships, you need to 'speak' the language of your partner. According to Gary, there are five languages we use:

- The first are the **words** of affirmation. These are the compliments, words of gratitude and just gentle words you use regarding your partner.

- Second is the quality of your **time** together. Some appreciate just being together, the presence of the other partner.

- Third is **touch**. Kinetically oriented people love being touched. Check if this is your partner's preference in communication. Normally this preference includes hugs, cuddles, making love and touching instead of words.

- Fourth is **giving gifts.** Some people want others to give gifts. It's an evolutionary need to be provided for and some have kept it until now.

- And the fifth is the **act of service**. 'Do it and I will feel better' type of thing. They want to see your actions, how you manifest your love in deeds. No words or cuddles help here, you need to move and do something to make them feel loved.

Taking the above into consideration, what are your preferences and what are your partner's? How can you give them more of what they want? The best thing to find out is to ask.

Story:

Maria comes to the therapy with tears in her eyes. Her boyfriend has been drinking, shouting and was even physically aggressive with her. She says she would leave him if only this was the first time, but her previous boyfriend had also behaved in a similar manner. She thinks something is wrong with her and she 'attracts' this type of men in her life.

After the first explorative session she discovers that she would attract men who at first would be seduced by her femininity but in time, would then be greeted by a very demanding woman who talked over them and tried to 'fix' them without respecting their decisions. Men she attracts want to hear words of affirmation as a love language whereas for her, love means service & gifts. She caters for them that means she loves them. Whereas the men she attracted wanted words of respect. Without respect, they felt cornered, powerless, and attended to their vice for release of stress. Once she understood this, she changed her behaviour and started becoming more aware of how she communicated with her current partner.

In the following session she mentioned she was surprised, as they both stopped shouting at each other and after three months he stopped binge-drinking. Their communication improved as well as their overall well-being.

Exercise 5. The air that we breathe and how we breathe it. When someone enters a panicked state, the people around them often say things like 'take a deep breath', and this is a good example of a suggestion to adopt a more useful physiological state. Deep breathing benefits the body greatly. Taking in more oxygen lowers blood pressure and relaxes muscles. It also relaxes the brain and causes the heart rate to slow down. Deep breathing helps our body to release more carbon dioxide. Among the many health benefits of deep breathing are its cleansing properties for the lymphatic system. We know that the lymph surrounds all the cells in our bodies, but a correct breathing technique can remove the toxins from these cells through the lymphatic system.

Deep breathing is known to release endorphins or so called 'feel-good hormones'. These are natural pain killers in the body and help relax the muscles and nerves. Deep breathing is also known to help people who are depressed. Asthmatics also benefit a lot from deep breathing as it makes the abdominal muscles stronger and improves the lung capacity. Shallow breathing leads to the flow of insufficient oxygen in the body which leads to muscle exertion, lethargy, and fatigue. Deep breathing can help us activate our relaxation stress relievers. It also helps people suffering from insomnia.

Story:

Marta suffers depression. Living in a small town where everyone knows everyone, she feels trapped. She does the job she knows how to do but she hates it the bottom of her heart. She loathes some people in her office but does not feel empowered to talk about it as she fears losing her job. Just before she decided to come to one of the ENRICHing workshops she finds out that her husband has secretly fathered another family over the previous 15 years. Shocked, devastated and perplexed she feels completely desperate.

I invite her to deepen her breathing as a daily practice. I also ask her to deep breath for as long as she can be mentally aware of. As soon as she starts implementing this ritual, I see a difference in her physiology, and she confirms the benefits by feeling a release of stress 'off her shoulders'. Her mimics change, her posture changes, her lips form the beginning of a smile. After the first session, she claims her sense of well-being has greatly improved, and has found a newfound strength to create a plan that can finally bring her passion to life – learning. Having two kids and needing to sort out double-family arrangements with her husband, she wants to follow her inner dream and begin learning new skills. She found a place in the big city to do that. She decided to buy a car and applied for a driver's licence. By simply following her dreams, Marta created positive energy inside which in turn helped her to deal with any stress from the outside. And all of this started from a mere breathing practice. Deep breathing. As Marta says, "that first little exercise of breathing was very powerful, and I now use it every time I feel stressed."

CHAPTER THREE

Respond vs. react

"It's not the situation, but whether we react negative or respond positive to the situation that is important."

\- Zig Ziglar

RESPONDING AND REACTING are very similar on the surface and even are considered synonymous in the English language, but they are two worlds apart when it comes to practice. Reacting is automatic, unconscious, and generally connected to the ancient reptilian part of our brain which we have retained as a mechanism to survive in dangerous situations. It is all about eliminating fear, and fear is connected to potential hazards. So, for example, in the past, if we were to notice a dangerous animal next to our baby, we would react very quickly by running, fighting, or freezing to save our life and the baby. This is useful and has developed in an evolutionary way, so we have this inheritance for good and for bad. For good because it keeps us safe from dangers when needed. But why for bad? Because reaction causes activation of the automatic processes and combined with hormonal changes, produces adrenalin and cortisol which are stress hormones. Cortisol is ok for a short period of time but becomes a rather nasty hormone if produced consistently in the body due to a prolonged stressful period.

In bad relationships, where stressful situations arise daily, the body becomes polluted with this hormone. It is produced by the adrenal gland in response to stress and it supresses the immune system. It also decreases bone formation. When people start suffering from colds and flu and think it is because of the weather, the truth is more likely it is because you have had too much stress and are having adrenalin gland fatigue due to chronic cortisol release.

Responding, in contrast, is a very advanced system that is the consciously developed area of our brains due to the growing role of the pre-frontal cortex. This part of our brain allows us to take control of our emotional responses and to choose which ones we want to have in any given moment. It is our 'navigation' system to healthier relationships. But we need to develop it because for some people, it hasn't been developed yet. The same applies to mammals. For some monkeys it is highly developed, and they use it to work out the best ways to operate in their group. For example, they may fight less and have healthier relationships. Others fight more and have social problems, and this is because there is a difference in the way their brain is developed. Pre-frontal cortex is considered nowadays, the most important part of the social brain, as it is linked to the social and emotional intelligence, which is crucial in how we operate in our day-to-day life.

Choosing your non-judgmental responses is critical for developing your pre-frontal cortex and in the long-term, in enriching relationships. Once the basics are sorted for nourishment of the body in terms of sleep, food, and shelter, then the emotional and mental levels of nourishment need to be satisfied with *responding* rather than *reacting*.

So here is another way to kick-start your new habits of responding well to your partner rather than reacting negatively or taking it personally.

Exercise 6. Body work to change your neurology. You know that if you change the way you move, you will change the way you feel. Notice, how you position your body when you feel bad and reactive. For example, think about when you are angry. Do it now, start feeling angry and notice the change in your body position. Generally, people tighten up, make fists, and close their arms in a crossed-arm position to their body or widen their elbows and place their fists on their hips to look more powerful. They start

frowning and tilt their head down, close their lips tight or display teeth to scare others off. Do whatever you do and acknowledge it, just by looking in the mirror. This is the body position when you feel angry.

Now, relax your body and look up smiling. Spread your arms and with open palms lift them high and open. Now breathe in deeply and breathe out. Stand up and do it again. Look up to the ceiling and smile, relax your face muscles and stay like this for two to three minutes. Now keeping this body and face position without changing muscles, try to get angry. You can't. The body and its physiology with the neurological connections that are made, will simply not allow you to feel angry nor sad. This is the quickest way to change your reactive pattern by taking control of your body. Change physiology, and you will change your psychology. Brilliant!

Story:

Irene approaches me after the last module of the ENRICHing workshop and shares a personal story. She is a single mother of a little boy. She asked her mother to look after the baby boy so she could come

55

to the workshop as she wanted to do something to find a new husband and build a better relationship with him. It turned out that after doing the Stance-Dance (moving from a stressed body postures to a more resourceful ones) she noticed how different her breathing was, how much lighter she felt, and she practiced this exercise at home before her previous husband came to play with their son. By surprise, when she opened the door and smiled standing with a different posture to what she would normally use to talk to him while he was visiting them, she shifted states not just for her but for him as well. Result? They decided to get back together. She was thrilled as in her heart she always loved him but couldn't cope with his womanising behaviour after the birth of their son. Apparently even his behaviour with other women has changed. She was both perplexed and excited about how a simple change of her body positioning could change her mood and therefore, change her relationship with her ex- husband.

CHAPTER FOUR

Imagine vs. will-power

> *"Imagination is the beginning of creation. You imagine what yoU desire, you will what you imagine and at last you create what you will."* - George Bernard Shaw

I LOVE JASMINE GREEN TEA. But what is so special in this drink that makes it so mesmerizing and captivating? I just want to enjoy it every morning after slowly waking up, especially on one of those crisp Autumnal days in October when the leaves are turning red and orange. I want to put on a warm robe and slippers and look outside the window at the beautiful mountains and forest and imagine I am there walking in the woods. I want to smell the still sleeping, lush, damp, green forest – that when woken by the sunshine – will become full of life and radiance and energy.

Is it the jasmine, or is it the warmth of the green tea leaves opening in the white china cup graciously moving around following the injection of the hot water? The water is about to boil and the excitement of having a cup of tea is growing inside of me. It provokes my imagination. What kind of tea am I going to have today? Mmmm...I always have something special for the morning when it's quiet and the people around me are still sleeping. I love this time of the day.

The taste is gorgeous. The smell is divine. The aftertaste is lingering for a while to remind me of the exquisite experience of the here and now, the one-on-one time with myself and my focusing my energy on the simple act of tea-drinking. Precious.

Just by reading this, you have imagined how it would feel to drink jasmine tea. Your taste buds and nostrils have already activated the neurons in your head of the olfactory areas which perceive smell and even the quantity and quality of your saliva has changed the taste in your mouth. If I were to put you in the MRI scanner, I would probably see the activation of the same regions in your brain as if you were drinking that tea. Your imagination is so powerful that you can create or destroy anything you want in life. This is especially so in your relationships.

Imagination is much more important and stronger than willpower, so here is an exercise to harness the skill of imagination.

Exercise 7. The first second of your day is the most important time. When you wake up and transport yourself from unconsciousness to consciousness, it is a magical moment. If you can tap into that space to expand it and make the best use of it, you can do wonders. Start imagining how you want to feel, what your organs would feel like and how you want to end

the day. It is a simple practice to transform your creativity and tap into your emotional imagination.

Story:

Molly suffers an overall tiredness. For a mother of three there is no time even to look after herself let alone reflect on how to improve her day. She is in serving mode to her family and falls asleep simply by throwing herself on a pillow, sometimes wearing the same clothes she has been in during the day. When she wakes up, she gathers her thoughts and continues a 'do-do' mode.

She finds out about the importance of a 'waking up moment' and decides to become aware of that precious little timeframe during her busy day. She wants to take advantage of the 'morning moment' to plan her day. But at first, it's tough. She either forgets about it or when she is fully awake, she finds herself already during the hectic morning schedule and inevitably being late for school and work.

But she perseveres, and slowly, day after day, she starts getting better at it. After a week of ups and downs, she begins to catch a glimpse of the feeling of being 'at one' with herself, of starting to feel 'whole'. Of being, not just doing. She enjoys this wonderful feeling and wants to enhance it more. There and then, she decides to sign up for a yoga class. Three months later, she decides to leave on a yoga retreat - to be on her own - and this has a profound effect on her. She later she confirms that all it was for her, was that sheer instant of waking up and being aware of herself. From that moment, her imagination took the lead, allowing her to create the desired outcome of the day and the feelings she wanted to experience. The day followed the mood and plans of her imagination.

CHAPTER FIVE

Communicate vs. assume

"Assumptions are the termites of relationships." - Henry Winkler

"To effectively communicate, we must realize that we are all different in the way we perceive the world and use this understanding as a guide to our communication with others." - Tony Robbins

COMMUNICATION TO RELATIONSHIPS is like breath to life', Virginia Satir used to say. I totally sign-up to this. How we communicate, and what we use as patterns for our communication is mainly learnt from the early ages: from parents, from school and from the TV & internet. If we want to change our patterns, we need to change our habits, and for that we need to change our actions. For actions to change, we need to change our thoughts. Does it sound a bit complicated? In fact, it's all simple and goes down to clear communication which is inside our head (thoughts) and outside our mouth (words). What is clear communication? It's when the other person understands your message the way you want them to. In communication it is also important to be non-judgemental. To stop thinking that someone is out there to 'get you,' or they do something because they don't like or love you, or they have something personal against you. In most cases they don't. Remember that in most cases people are busy thinking about themselves and worrying about their own stuff rather than yours. To help you clear out your own thoughts and get on a path of clear communication, I have picked a great exercise here.

Exercise 8. Positivity rocks! No-one can get enough of positive vibes - especially when most of the news and

stories out there are negative. There is an abundance of research in this field. Personally, what helps me step into a positive mood every day is a simple routine that involves only five minutes of my time daily but saves a lot of nerve cells afterwards. The essence is simple; remember and say, '3 positive things from the previous day'.

When I wake up, I think of three things that happened the day before that were amazing. It can be as small and simple as appreciating someone's help or cooking a lovely dinner. I then say them to my partner or write (even better) these three things and send them to him via email or text message. He in turn responds and sends his own '3 positive things' and hey presto, the day is immediately off to a better start! What this whole experience does is place me in an invisible radio station that is tuned to positive, and I instantly start producing the love hormone, oxytocin. This not only helps me throughout the first couple of hours of the day, but turns into a positive inertia afterwards, which is both natural and extremely fulfilling!

TRY THIS: When you wake up, think and exchange three positive things that happened the day before.

Story:

Silvia and Robert haven't had sex for four months although they sleep in the same bed and have been married for two years now. Silvia wants to get pregnant, but Robert thinks they can wait for a couple of years. She decides to check in with a psychologist to understand what she can do -as she is emotionally upset and has moments of extreme panic. These anxious moments are normally the time when she then lets Robert know all about his 'drawbacks' and 'faults'. He withdraws and sometimes sleeps in a different room.

My first question is regarding their communication when they wake up in the morning. Apparently, it's predictably the same. Silvia shows she is upset that they didn't have sex. Rob quickly gets ready and goes to work with almost no talking.

I ask Silvia to start with a small change of their daily routine. And instead of leaving for work on that note, start with the '3 positive exercise' when they wake up and only talk about positive things that happened during the previous day.

Finding it difficult at first, Silvia manages to collect three positive things to share with Rob the following morning and writes them down. She sends him an email with this subject line: '3 positive things that happened yesterday'. And here is what she mentions:

1. There was sunshine during the day, and I really liked it. I remembered when you brought flowers just because it was a sunny day.
2. I thank you for being with me even though at times I behave so emotionally.
3. I finished one more presentation.

After a week of sending these small messages - ranging from saying she liked something Rob did during the day or sharing a special memory with him from the past, not only made them feel closer to each other but they simply re-connected again.

CHAPTER SIX

HUGS & HUMOUR vs. withdraw

"You need three hugs a day to
survive, six hugs to maintain a
normal life, and twelve hugs a
day to thrive" - V. Satir

HUGGING HAS A LOT OF BENEFITS. We connect with the person so intimately when we hug because we touch heart to heart. The proximity allows for personalisation and that makes some changes in the chemical balance of our body. Our blood gets flooded with oxytocin, the hugging hormone, and we feel safer, secure, trusting, caring as well as cared for. It is a free miracle we can exercise every day of our life.

Olga's favourite time is when she wakes up being hugged by her beloved man. That does not happen often as they travel to different places. But when they are in the same house she prefers to start the day with that combined energy, feeling deeply connected to him, feeling loved, supported and cared for.

They have a few rules in their family regarding hugging:

- They sleep & hug together (when they are in the same house).
- They resolve any negative issues before going to bed.
- They wake up and do physical exercises together in the morning (at least 5 minutes).
- They say '3 positive things' that happened the day before to each other first thing in the morning.

All this helps them hug and feel good about each other and it is a wonderful way to start a beautiful day!

Olga's best substitute for hugging her man is a hug of her children. They hug every morning. They hug every time they leave for school and when she picks them up. They hug before they go to bed and of course they hug a lot during the day. She says 'I love you' many times a day to them just because she wants them to know that she loves them no-matter-what. She believes it is important to say this out loud to them. She says it, not only when they do something good or behave the way she wants them to, but just at random times throughout the day when nothing happens, and she just has some time with them to say it. Normally, when she drives a car or sits down with them, she physically lowers herself to their level and looks at them eye-to-eye. She will say, "Do you know how much I love you? I love you so much and so strong. Like an elephant hug." And they hug. And her little one says, "Mom, I love you so much like from here to Mars." They continue this game of 'how much I love you'. It's fun and they hug a lot.

For hugs there are a lot of wonderful exercises but the main one is just hugging. Easy, ah? As soon as we become aware of the benefits of hugs, we reach for a hug naturally.

Exercise 9. Hug twelve times a day. Virginia Satir used to say: 'We need 3 hugs a day to survive, 8 hugs a day to maintain a good balance and 12 hugs to thrive'. Try it and feel the difference. There are some hug therapy groups where people can go just to have hugs[ii], but you can just enjoy the free ones from your family, your friends and even your colleagues.

Story:

When Vanessa worked in a big corporation, she used to greet people with a hug, especially if she hasn't seen them for a while. She knew from reading on their face that they liked it. They were smiling and their posture changed to be more relaxed, and they would take a big breath.

***

Hugging is fun, healthy and it is the best remedy for depression, emotional swings, and low self-esteem. After hugging twelve times, you will feel you are more lovable, more energetic and fuller of a positive upward spiral that will see you through the busy week ahead and emotional rollercoasters of your daily life.

Humour vs. withdraw

"Your sense of humour is one of the most powerful tools you have to make certain that your daily mood and emotional state support good health." -
Paul E. McGhee, Ph.D.

Laughter is a powerful antidote to stress, pain, and conflict. Nothing works faster or more effectively to bring your mind and body back into balance than a good laugh. Humour is great in relationships as it lightens your thoughts, inspires hopes, connects you to others, and keeps you focused on the bigger picture.

Laughter is known to have power to heal and renew cells. It has a tremendous ability to enhance your relationships and support both physical and emotional health.

These are some of its benefits.[iii]

Physical Health Benefits:

- Boosts immunity
- Lowers stress hormones
- Decreases pain
- Relaxes your muscles
- Prevents heart disease

Mental Health Benefits:

- Adds joy and zest to life
- Eases anxiety and fear
- Relieves stress
- Improves mood
- Enhances resilience

Social Benefits:

- Strengthens relationships
- Attracts others to us
- Enhances teamwork
- Helps defuse conflict
- Promotes group bonding

Exercise 10. Here is a list of other ideas for making space for fun and laughter in your relationships. I hope you enjoy and do let me know how you are getting on after trying them!

Laughter Tips for Relationships [iv]

1. Laugh together for 2-3 min each morning.

2. Laugh together for 2-3 min each evening before going to sleep.

3. Have fun when you have sex

4. Send funny messages to each other at least one per day.

5. Have a laughter match to see who can laugh loudest and longest.

6. Surround yourself with flowers. "The earth laughs in flowers." - Emerson.

7. Have a competition who can find the funniest story during the day.

8. Start a diary of anecdotes and funny stories and read them to each other.

9. List the positive things in your day each day and read them to each other.

10. Play together one hour a week. Examples: Sing, dance, race each other, give exaggerated hugs, count smiling faces when driving together.

Story:

Melissa has been in a relationship with Keith for thirteen years. They had their ups and downs and now are in a stable but distant stage of apathy. Both are feeling withdrawn from each other.

Nothing seems to bring fun and joy in their relationship. They spend more and more time apart, often with other people.

They have a lot at stake including children, properties, and mutual dreams they had built together. But they still want to be together. They agree to revive their partnership and try and rekindle that passion and love again.

They are given a task to do; complete the above list of ten activities daily for at least one week and then report back any changes in behaviour they have seen between them.

One week later they come back with their findings. The fact that they both wanted this to work and changes to happen allowed them to connect and become a team again. They had fun. A lot of fun. They liked laughing and remembering funny stories they used to tell each other. It revived their intimacy. It allowed them to feel closer and passionate again. They did not want to leave the house to spend time with friends as before. They wanted to stay together. Their kids noticed a difference in their communication and laughed with them.

***

As we have seen, there are a lot of benefits from laughing. Laughter decreases stress hormones and increases immune cells and infection-fighting antibodies, thus improving your resistance to disease. Laughter triggers the release of endorphins, the body's natural feel-good chemicals. Endorphins promote an overall sense of well-being and can even temporarily relieve pain.

Laughter is a strong medicine not just for mind and body but for relationships as well. Even when people have a terrible fight, my best recommendation would be to imagine 10 years from now. Would they laugh at the current situation? In many cases, they start smiling when just thinking about it!

Looking forward looking back

I'm looking forward to the future, and feeling grateful for the past. - Mike Rowe

WAKING UP EARLY AND GOING FOR A RUN is a present Ana gives to herself. It is a special time of the day when nature conspires to help her with her purpose in life. When people around her are still sleeping, she is expanding time to connect with herself and the universe. Ana uses this time to get answers to her questions and transform those dark parts of hers into light.

She loves having a moment for herself and especially when she feels her body releasing endorphins and dopamine. She loves running, jogging, yoga, swimming, bathing, or any physical activity in nature.

Nature is so important as it allows us to breathe in fresh air. When we breathe in air, we breathe in life and information for our unconsciousness. That's why it's so important when Ana wants to be creative, she goes outside. She opens the window. She goes outdoors. She has a walk to breathe in fresh air and stay tuned to her inner self.

On one of those beautiful mornings, she went for a run along a small river in Geneva, Switzerland, at the beginning of Spring 2015. As she was passing the trees she thought, 'These wonderful big trees are supporting me so well and thanks to them I feel a lot of energy, breathing in the fresh, crisp, morning air.' There was no one else there, just her, and she loved that time. She could shout and laugh, and no one was listening. So, she did. She was looking at the river and saw clear water running and leaving the stones underneath beautiful, grounded, and tranquil – it was like a river of life. As the river was turning to the right, she noticed that some of its water was following the flow, and some was stuck in a bay area. The stuck water was twirling around creating froth and collecting leaves, debris and even some rubbish. This disheartened Ana. She wanted to pass that part quickly and not investigate it as to her, it appeared dirty and ugly. That reminded Ana of a time when she felt trapped in life. That was a time when she felt stuck - at home, at work, and in a relationship that was neither changing nor fulfilling, she was locked in a routine which offered no light at the end of the tunnel. She passed that 'ugly part,' happily following the flow of clear water that was running and turning and following the river of life. The next part was also fascinating for her. Something suddenly attracted her attention to the point that she had to stop and listen. She saw that water was flowing through big stones creating a small waterfall and this was the sound that stopped her in her tracks. Ana stood stationary and looked into what was probably the most beautiful creation of water and rock: waterfalls. Water falling from a challenging part of its path and overcoming obstacles - which were rocks. This was suddenly the most glorious part of the river. Her mind helped connect the dots and it opened her understanding of how beautiful all challenges, painful bits and struggles are for our soul. There will always be adversity, but it is up to us to make ourselves beautiful and free.

***

Thank you for reading, I truly hope you find my findings insightful and the exercises helpful. These learnings from the book can be further enhanced when combined with the ENRICH YOUR RELATIONSHIPS Programme. I also run a variety of workshops and courses as well as individual coaching – all details can be found at www.daryahaitoglou.com. I would love to hear your comments and if you have experienced any changes or results after reading this book – feel free to email me at darya@enrich.global

For now, I will leave you with these wonderful quotes. Thank you and stay enriched!

> *The Family is the vehicle from whom we learn to be who we are.* – Virginia Satir

> *We either make ourselves miserable, or we make ourselves strong, the amount of work is the same.* – Carlos Castaneda

Growth and learning can come from any situation or experience, problem, or crisis. — Virginia Satir

Life is between what you desire most and what you fear most. — Tony Robbins

Once a human being has arrived on this earth, communication is the largest single factor determining what kinds of relationships he or she makes with others and what happens to him in the world about him. — Virginia Satir

ENRICH questionnaire

PART 1.

1. Has it been a long time since you had passionate, deeply connected intimacy with your partner?

   Yes/No

2. Do you feel you are bored in your intimate life with your partner now?

   Yes/No

3. Do you tend to follow a routine when you are intimate with your partner?

   Yes/No

   ⇨ If you answered *Yes* to more than one of these questions, go to Chapter 1 of the book, to transform yourself from a **'routine junkie'** to a **'genius explorer'**.

PART 2.

4.   Do you feel you over-give to your partner in your intimate life?

Yes/No

5.   Do you hide your disappointment when you don't like sex you had?

Yes/No

6.   Do you normally serve your partner only, despite your own needs?

Yes/No

7.   Do you feel you don't get enough quantity or quality sex from your partner?

Yes/No

⇨   If you answered Yes to more than one of these questions, go to Chapter 2 of the book, to transform yourself from a '**depleted care-giver**'/ '**grumpy demander**' to a '**nourishing lover**'.

PART 3.

8. When you feel disappointed, do you tend to blame your partner (even inside your head)?
   Yes/No

9. Do you tend to take a blame on yourself and ask for another chance?
   Yes/No

10. Do you tend to switch topics when it gets to sex?
    Yes/No

11. Do you tend to start being quiet when your partner starts talking about intimacy with you?
    Yes/No

12. Do you accuse your partner of not talking about your intimate moments?

Yes/No

⇨ If you answered *Yes* to at least one of these questions, go to Chapter 3 of the book, to transform yourself from a '**reactive agent**' to a '**responding angel**'.

PART 4.

13. Do you try to prove your point of view to your partner so he/she understands?

Yes/No

14. Do you find yourself in a power-struggle with your partner about even tiny things?

Yes/No

15. Do you tend to switch topics when it gets to sex?

Yes/No

16. Is sex a matter of persistence to do it more often?

Yes/No

17. Do you find your partner is tired of spending time with you recently?

Yes/No

⇨ If you answered *Yes* to at least one of these questions, go to Chapter 4 of the book, to transform yourself from a '**nerve-wrecker**' to a '**loving magician**'.

PART 5.

18. When you don't understand why things go the way they go, do you rather keep silent assuming you know why?

Yes/No

19. Has it been a long time since you talked openly about your sex preferences?

Yes/No

20. Do you find yourself talking to yourself or your friends about your intimate relationships rather than to your partner?
Yes/No

21. Do you tend to take things personally if you don't have a deep connection with your partner?
Yes/No

22. Do you think you can mind-read?
Yes/No

⇨ If you answered *Yes* to at least one of these questions, go to Chapter 5 of the book, to transform yourself from a '**hopeless mind-reader**' to a '**communication master** '.

PART 6.

23. In a difficult situation, do you tend to shut down emotionally, processing it internally?

Yes/No

24. Do you tend to stop talking to your partner when you feel uncomfortable?

Yes/No

25. Do you tend to move away and reject him/her in sex when you feel upset?

Yes/No

26. Do you find yourself withdrawing from a difficult discussion with your partner?

Yes/No

27. Do you tend to procrastinate talking to your partner about issues you seem to have?

Yes/No

⇨ If you answered yes to at least one of these questions, go to Chapter 6 of the book, to transform yourself from a **'kind stone-waller'** to a **'lover with a twist'**.

Footnotes

[i] http://www.therichest.com/rich-list/world/worlds-10-most-divorced-nations/2/

[ii] http://www.cuddletherapy.com/

[iii] http://www.helpguide.org/articles/emotional-health/laughter-is-the-best-medicine.htm

[iv] https://www.laughtertherapy.com/laughter-tips/laughter-tips-for-relationships

About the Author:

Darya Haitoglou, BA(Hons), MSc(Dist), MPhil, BScPsy, MTNLP

Psychologist and Relationship Coach

Darya has a passion to help people fulfil their potential and be the best they can. Throughout her experience of being a full-time working mum, a student, a coach, and a leader in multi-national corporations, she has found a simple way of helping people raise their self-esteem and get the relationships and life they want.

After graduating with First Class Honours in Economics followed by a Masters' of Philosophy from Cambridge University, Darya went to Japan to study cross-cultural management. Later she returned to the UK and studied psychology while working for eight years in Marketing & Human Resources for a large global company. There she trained coaches to fulfil their potential and be the best they could.

Darya has a private coaching practice and creates and conducts life events, workshops, and retreats as part of the Enrich Your Relationships Programme.

PRAISE

"Darya's seminar changed my life. It triggered a deep self-examination which, over the following 3 days, made me realize and acknowledge the habits, attitudes and approaches that had led to my previous relationship problems and lack of self-esteem. Now I am clear on what needs to change, and I am absolutely committed to giving myself the huge gift that success would represent. And if that all sounds a bit intense, let me assure you that the seminar was great fun as well!" – **Malcolm** Clarke, Finance Director, Europe, India, Middle East & Africa, Procter & Gamble

"Enrich" is the right word! I find Darya very interesting because she works on so many different levels and yet they all seem to fit together in the human jigsaw puzzle of a personality. Her workshop was totally different to any other. She brings you through a completely different way of approach which allowed me to discover my own personality through fun 'Physical Interactive Play roles'. On reflection, this process clearly resonated with me to understand some of the key elements to my personality. It was very powerful and I cannot wait for the next workshop. – **Melanie** Watters – Designer & Founder, Lemiena London

"I honestly feel so lucky I have met Darya and that I participated in the Enrich your Relationships Programme. Darya is a wise woman that exhales love and light! Her workshop could be described as a concentrated and wonderfully combined programme of different methods of psychology- as an extension and effect of the wisdom she has acquired during her long way of inner development. The result ends up being so strong and powerful that your heart starts to sing the very primary melody of our uncovered emotions, allowing us to align with every human being. The experience is catalytic and I recommend it to all those who are not afraid to watch, to listen to, to hold, to speak and to feel, to walk in the paths of the soul, to explore themselves, to feel their existence as one and therefore unite with the others. A very big thanks Darya from the bottom of my heart!!" – **Georgia** Papadimitriou, HR Manager, OTE Group (Organisation of Telecommunications in Greece)

"I believed I had an open heart and I thought I was able to reason well with everyday difficulties I faced. However, I realised how much more I was capable of when I had worked through this enriching relationships workshop. I saw how much more I was capable of. I begin to recognize just how well I could cope with situations, feelings and dealing with matters that cause difficulties emotionally and mentally. I was more energised and became armed with so much more than I thought possible. Sharing, understanding, laughing and listening – it was a pleasure to take part in during this workshop. The workshop was run at a great pace with plenty of time to reflect, it felt safe and comfortable. The venue setting was beautiful, inspiring and very calming which mirrored the energy of the day. I now see that I have even more to learn and understand, but I will achieve this through further workshops that Darya will be running" – **Sophie** Hollyoak, Mother of Annabelle & Eloise.

"Darya's training has been an intense, emotional and experiential day! I have learnt new things about building relationships with people and I feel enriched by the connections we have made. Darya is a fantastic facilitator, empathic and knowledgeable" – **Luigi**i Matrone, eBusiness Institute Founder

"I really enjoyed the workshop "Enrich your Relationships" because it allowed me to empower myself with practical and positive exercises. Darya is a caring teacher that will make you feel safe and secure during the workshop, therefore you will be able to open your heart and mind. I am looking forward for the next workshop!" – **Claudine** Audibert – Artist & Painter

"Such a wonderful and enriching experience which has helped me grow. I would highly recommend to others" – R**achel** Volpicelli - Mother of Charlotte & Mathilde.

Printed in Great Britain
by Amazon